C000069892

Life-Shift
Experiences

The moral and social impact of a (non) chosen death

Ten personal Life-Shift stories

Ofkje Teekens & Kees Paling

Copyright © 2020 Ofkje Teekens & Kees Paling

All rights reserved.

ISBN: 9798562652973

Independently published

DEDICATION

We dedicate this book to the authors who had
the courage to share their story with the world.
And to all volunteers in the world who work
day and night to prevent suicide attempts.

CONTENTS

ACKNOWLEDGMENTS

We want to thank everybody who contributed to this book.

We really hope these stories will make a difference.

INTRODUCTION

Of the several collections of Life-Shift Stories we
published, this is the first one that will be devoted entirely
to one special, very serious theme: *suicide*.

In 2019, at a conference in the South of France, we heard
the testimonials of two brave men who survived their own
suicide attempt. Since then, they are on a mission to
prevent other people of walking into this same dark, dead-
end street. We are proud to have one of them – Rob
Goddard – in this book.

After the testimonials, it turned out there were more people
at the conference who had experienced the moral and social
impact of a (non) chosen death: they had lost a family
member or a friend to suicide and they still felt the pain.
Listening to these stories, we decided to collect some of
these experiences in a book, to make readers aware of,
understand and feel the consequences of such an
irreversible act.

Suicide has become a major health problem in the world
today. As the World Health Organization (WHO) states:
every 40 seconds somebody, somewhere in this world, dies

from suicide. And for every suicide-death there are twenty suicide-attempts.

There are a lot of differences between countries. Although almost 80% of all suicides occurred in low- and middle-income countries, the high-income countries (Europe, USA) had the highest rate of more than 11 suicides per 100.000. Among young adults (15-30) suicide is the second leading cause of death, after road injury. And in the high-income countries, three times as many men as women die by suicide.

In this book we present ten stories of people who experienced the struggle with depression and suicidal thoughts themselves, or who were witness to the dark thoughts and fears of a parent, a sibling, a friend or a colleague.
These are poignant stories of courageous people who decided to share their experiences for the benefit of the world. We are very grateful for that and we think you are all wonderful people. Bless you!

Ofkje Teekens & Kees Paling

(Two of the authors use a pseudonym to protect the privacy of their families).

1

SOMEWHERE A STAR SHINES FOR US

"I am sitting on my cloud
And am happy to see
Down below a beautiful girl is born
So sweet and cute

I will watch over you
My dear baby sister
Every night before you go to sleep
I will throw you a small kiss from heaven"

Robbe

By Carol Bailleul

This small poem figures on the birth card of our daughter
Ellen. Ellen has just turned eighteen, but as you may have

already guessed, she was not our firstborn child. Our firstborn was a baby boy named Robbe.

The Verdict

Let us go back in time to the moment when we found out that Robbe would never be an ordinary boy. I remember that day like it was yesterday. Thursday, June 14, 2001. My husband and I were on holiday in Italy. Touring with our motorhome. The phone rang. It was our gynaecologist. Bad news. A recent blood test indicated possible abnormalities in the foetus. The doctor insisted on doing an amniocentesis as quickly as possible.

Devastated we rushed back home. The weeks that followed were lived as in a nightmare. After the diagnosis of Down syndrome with possible cardiac abnormalities everything was arranged for me to be hospitalised for the termination of the pregnancy.

Indeed, before the pregnancy my husband and I had agreed to terminate the pregnancy in case of serious disabilities. This had been a heart wrenching, but a considered and thoughtful decision taking into account the well-being of us as a couple and of our future children. Neither of us felt capable of caring for a child with special needs.

However, no matter how many times we had discussed this before, no matter how much we were convinced about the rightness of our decision, now that we actually got the bad news, it still felt like choosing between bad and worse. Under these circumstances there is no such thing as a good decision.

Besides the fact that as a parent you feel awful when facing the death of your child, you are confronted with a lot of rejection in your environment. Voluntary pregnancy termination is a taboo. A lot of people don't understand and don't want to talk about it. As a result, losing your baby is something you often have to deal with alone as a couple. Fortunately, times have changed and the network of available psychological support has increased immensely during the last decade.

Almost 20 years later I must confess that losing a baby is without doubt one of the most traumatic experiences to endure.

Birth

So, on July 3rd 2001 our son was born. It was all rather surreal. Delivery being started ... Giving birth to a child of which I knew he wouldn't survive the power of the contractions ... Holding the foetus in my arms only for a short while ... Being taken to the operating room with urgency to have the placenta removed ... Returning home without baby ... Pleading with the municipality to get a tombstone for our son ... Seeing my husband create a little coffin to burry our son ... The burial with just the two of us...

Mourning

The first two weeks after the burial I lived on autopilot. I cannot even remember how I came through those days. The only thing I remember is that I visited the grave every day. It was something I simply had to do. As if I hoped that all of a sudden I would wake up and find out that it was all just a bad nightmare ...

I wrote a poem in memory of Robbe and created an album with the screenshots of the ultrasound and the only picture we got from Robbe just after birth, taken by the hospital nurse. I needed a tangible reminder of my baby. Years later,

I often regretted that we hadn't taken any more pictures of Robbe together with us as a family. We were so ignorant and overwhelmed at the time.

Then, suddenly, after two weeks things clicked and I picked up my daily routine. Time to move on. Slowly I resumed my business activities. In the meantime my husband and I had our blood samples analysed to make sure that nothing was genetically wrong. Good news! Statistics had been against me. One out of thousand women risks having a disabled baby.

This news was very important to us because it meant that we could become pregnant again and have a healthy baby after all.

The second pregnancy

From that moment onwards I was obsessed with getting pregnant again. It was as if we had to prove something to our environment and to ourselves. Five months later I got pregnant again.

If you thought that I would be walking on clouds from that moment onwards, then I must disappoint you. The second pregnancy was the most stressful pregnancy a parent can have. There is this constant fear that something might go wrong. It was logical this time to have an amniocentesis done to check if the baby was okay. Luckily, after a couple of days of waiting and worrying, we got the reassuring call: Our baby was as healthy as could be! It was a baby girl. We were over the moon!

From that moment we could start enjoying the pregnancy, buying baby stuff and making plans for the future of our daughter. However, we never completely relaxed. We were closely monitored by the doctor and upon the slightest belly ache no risks were taken and we had to check in at the hospital.

On the day when the contractions started, things could still go for the worst. The baby wouldn't come naturally and all of a sudden an emergency caesarian was necessary. On top of all this stress the doctor couldn't give me any additional anesthetic for the sake of the baby. So, I suffered and felt every action of the doctor. Then, finally, after almost 24 hours of labour, our daughter was born on September 15, 2002. We named her Ellen.

Rainbow Baby

We were very happy with our baby daughter, but somehow I couldn't really enjoy motherhood.

Maybe I worried that happiness for the second baby would look like treason towards the first baby? It was all very confusing at the time. Is it possible to feel happiness and sadness at the same time?

What is also difficult is that the outside world sees you as a first-time mother, while you are not. Yet, the story of the first child often goes unnoticed and this hurts.

Ellen cried a lot and we were exhausted. I have never been diagnosed with postpartum depression, but I am convinced now that I was very close to one if this wasn't already the case.

Ellen grew up with a sensitive respiratory system. We had to visit a doctor at least once a month. Moreover, she appeared to be a crybaby. The exhaustion of the first three years made us decide that one baby was enough. We couldn't cope with another stressful pregnancy and crybaby!

I wish I had known then what we found out about 9 years

ago: Our girl was very special, very gifted and overexcited. If we had known from the very beginning, we could have given her the care she needed.

As a small child we took Ellen to the cemetery to greet her brother. She hadn't known him, but she believed him to watch over her from up above. There he was, a special star shining for us.

As years go by, the memory of our loss faded. Sometimes we were reminded of our son. Every year on his day of birth my husband and I celebrate that we are his parents.

One Child Missing

In the early years after Ellen's birth, when someone asked me how many children I had, I answered "One.", but somehow it didn't feel right. After a couple of years, though, I decided to answer "Two.", because this is exactly how it feels: We have a family with two children, a boy and a girl. As a matter of fact, I didn't want our son to be forgotten. On the contrary, the more years that passed, the more I felt the need to make it visible that we also had a son.

When we moved 13 years ago, the one thing I missed the most, was the fact that I couldn't visit our son's grave any longer. We live about 90 kilometers from the town where our son was buried.

When I was recovering from a burnout in 2011, I made several life changing decisions. One of them was to have our son reburied in our new town. It was a huge administrative burden to get this arranged. And it cost us a lot of money. However, it was worth the effort. We bought a tomb for the three of us: my husband, our son, and myself, so that our daughter wouldn't have to worry about that when we died. We have the possibility again to visit the grave as much as we want to. It was such a relief for me, and necessary to be able to move forward.

Insights

If I were to relive the same issue again, there are certain things that I would do differently.

First of all, I would spend more time with the baby after birth. I would have a lot of pictures taken. The only memory we have now is the one picture taken by the nurse. In those days psychological support was still in its infancy, but it is of utmost importance. Talking about the pain of a lost child can help to find a haven for one's sorrow.

Personally, I used my talents as a writer and an artist to deal with my pain. I wrote a poem, put a little scrapbook together, and looked for support groups of parents who lost a child just like us. I told the story over and over again to friends and family. It was very important for me not to hide this story, but to unveil it whenever relevant.

This is one of the lessons that I learned from this experience: The loss of our child will always leave a scar, but scars do heal. This scar may be visible as it is a typical characteristic of myself and my life story. This experience has made me who I am.

An impact that I could never have foreseen is how the death of a child affects the life of the child who comes next. The grief over the loss of the first baby and the constant worrying during the second pregnancy are negative feelings leading to stress. These feelings are unconsciously transmitted to the foetus. A heavy load to carry for the rainbow baby. I have realized this in the meantime.

I have a message for every parent who experiences the loss of a child: Please accept how you feel. There is no right or wrong. Everything is okay. Please try to integrate the baby you lost into your family. Give yourself time to do so. Forgive yourself and be patient with yourself.

If you feel the need to share your story or are looking for support, there are several lovely initiatives for parents who have lost their children. They can be found in every country. Here are some references for Belgium and The Netherlands: www.cozapo.org and www.scwb.nl

Furthermore, I would be more than happy to welcome you personally as well as in my retreat house along the coast. We can share our thoughts in all discretion over a heartwarming cup of tea.

Let me finish this story in the way I started it: With a poem. I would like to share with you the poem that I wrote shortly after the death of our son. This was my way to deal with this loss ...

Full of excitement we looked at your first images.
It was love at first sight!
You were so beautiful, so lively and cute.
Simply wonderful!
You kept on tumbling and turning your little fingers.

As if you couldn't get enough of it!
Yes, you definitely enjoyed your time in my belly.
We were so proud of you!
We had made all kinds of plans for you.
Your teddies were waiting to welcome you home.

But then,
Out of the blue
We got this terrible news ...
We would never see you grow up.
We would never hug you.
It simply wasn't meant to be.
Even worse, you weren't meant to be ...

Ruthlessly you were taken from us.
Leaving us orphaned.
All that was left, was emptiness and pain.
One last look.
One last hug.
Before you left us for ever.
There you were, together with teddy,
On your way to the Kingdom of Angels.

Even though we had to let you go,
We will never forget you, Robbe.
We belong together,
Daddy, you and me.
In our hearts you will always be with us
And we will always love you.

Born in 1968 in the city of Ypres, world renowned for its battles "In Flanders' Fields" during the First World War, Carol settled by the sea together with her husband Diederik and daughter Ellen some twelve years ago.

After a long career in international companies, amongst others in managerial functions, Carol made an important life shift after a burnout and became a transformational coach and teacher.

She founded her own company called "Sharwa" together with her husband Diederik. Sharwa means "sherpa" in Sherpa language. Following the example of the sherpa in the Himalayan mountains, Carol will guide you along your personal journey to the top of the mountain.

2

FORGET YOUR EGO, WORK HARD AND BE FREE

By Olivier Barbarin

I was born in 1970 in the South of France. I was the second child of my parents; I have a sister who is four years older.

As a child, at the age of nine, I was a genius. I excelled in everything; at school, but also in sports. For instance: When I played soccer with my team, I used to score ten or twelve goals per game.

I became so strong, that it turned against me: It became a nightmare, because my first and biggest opponent was my own father. He couldn't handle me being a genius.

I became a target, I became the enemy.

This all started when I was around nine years old.

Control and confidence

It made me lose my confidence. When you love yourself and you have confidence, you can achieve anything. But my father destroyed my confidence, and my mother's and my sister's.

He wanted to keep everything under control, including our personalities. You couldn't have ideas of your own; he didn't allow you to have them. At that time my father was in his late thirties.

My father had a medical profession; he was a kinesiologist. He had his own practice.

But it wasn't until after his death that we found out he had committed fraud. For more than ten years he had been writing false invoices, that he sent to the French National Social Security. One year before his death, they discovered this fraud and they told him he would lose his job and maybe end up in prison.

Neither my mother nor my sister, nor I knew of my father's fraud. I was almost 21 years old, and in my last year at the university at the time. I had left the house when I was 18.

Fraud and adultery

My father had a double life. Not only was he committing fraud in his work; for three years he had been seeing another women too.

He didn't love himself, and, at that moment, he was losing everything. He lost control, he felt empty inside and in the end he was suffering all day.

As I see it today: when that is your situation, you don't have a choice. It's too much at the same time for one human being. It's too much pressure.

In the end he also learned he had cancer. And I really believe you create your own disease. It's true.

Nobody knew he had cancer. Of course, he had friends, but not really close friends.

I think he was alone. He didn't know how to be happy.

My mother didn't know about the cancer either. She was too kind and too much under control. Later, my mother told us that when my sister was three years old, she wanted to leave my father. But, in the end, she stayed because of my sister and me.

That was wrong, of course. It's better to break up and be free than stay in a bad marriage.

Mother's love

My mother is still alive, she is 74 now. But she's living with her regrets. As children we received much love from our mother: She was very kind. But she didn't get much love from my father, so she was heart-broken.
She never really recovered.

Unfortunately, my sister repeated my parent's marriage. She's in her fifties now and as a couple they are more conscious now and find a way to live together more harmoniously.

For me the key is 'conscious'. You need to put conscious first.

They have a wonderful boy, who is a teenager now. Together, they found their answers and it's more peaceful now. They saved their marriage.

I do not have a family myself, because I was on my inside journey. It was my destiny to live that way. I discovered meditation and many other things, because I was curious about that. I had many adventures with women, but my priority was to be free. That was my goal.

I need to be connected to my heart, to my feelings, my intuition, my instincts. And every day I have to live in the present moment.

Live in the moment

The past didn't exist, it's too late. The future doesn't exist, it didn't happen. So you can only live 100% in the present moment. That is the only truth and the only way to live consciously. It's all about energy and intensity. Forget your head, forget your ego. You don't need them, you only need your heart.

When a new baby is growing, the first that appears is the heart. Because the heart is the key to being human. So, forget your ego, forget the look of others. You don't need their approval.

What you need to ask yourself is: How can I be happy during the day? If you do that, you can be open to everything in this life: To nature, to the animals, to others, to humanity in general. It's easy!

If you do not know yourself, love yourself, it's impossible to be open-hearted. I discovered all this and now I live this mantra, because it IS a mantra.

I want to share this with everybody, because if you live this way, everything is possible.

You can achieve all your goals, because you are free.

I read it in his eyes

The last time I saw my father, I was almost 21. I saw my father, I looked in his eyes and I knew: This is the last time you see your father. He had made his decision, he knew it would happen within a few days. And I knew without any information: My intuition, my instincts told me: This is the last time. He said goodbye, without words, but I read it in his eyes.

If you listen to your instincts, they will tell you the truth – every day.

It made me sad, of course. But I believe, if someone has made that decision, like he did, you don't have the power to change it. Nobody has, I'm sure of that. My father was no longer happy in this world. Life for him had become a nightmare and he was only suffering.

He didn't talk about these things, these feelings. In fact, he never shared anything with anybody. And if you do that, it's really over. It's your own sentence; you feel alone. You are alone.

In the beginning we all felt guilty - my mother, my sister, and I. What you need to do, is to find out what happened and why it happened. You do research like a journalist. What happened in my family? Not only with my parents, but also with my grandparents. You will have to analyze that, in a psychological way.

Where did our journey take us, that in the end a family member would take his own life?

I now understand, because on my own journey I found my answers and that made me free.
And as soon as I was free, I no longer felt guilty.

The Matrix

Of course, I sought a professional to help me. She was a great lady, who directly understood. She said that I was brave and courageous and that I would get over it, but that it would take two years. And so it was.

I have never had depressive feelings myself, because I was conscious. I'm in love with life and I love myself. I'm very proud of what I've done. You need to reset your whole life, like in the movie 'The Matrix'.

You need to get really inside yourself and that takes courage. But the prize is unbelievable, as you become free to live as you wish. It is possibly not the only way to do it; the solution is to find your answers. If you cannot find your answers, you cannot do it.

So: don't give up; you need to believe you have the power to change things. Stop your suffering; be brave, be courageous, and put all your emotions on the table. Work hard, don't give up, because it's the only way to become free. Work on this every day and everyday things will become more clear. You will feel the change and the progress you make.

I used to be a sports producer and I was lucky to have met Michael Jordan, Zinedine Zidane, Rafael Nadal and Roger Federer. These kind of men – you cannot imagine how complete they are. They have the answers every day, not only in sports, but in life too.

They don't need anything, they don't need anyone; they need to be in their own matrix.

Go for it

I wasn't in top-sports myself, but I understood how it worked. If you are confident and know yourself, you can do it. And if you have any fear, you go for it, you face it. If you are afraid of something, it is interesting. And you go for it: Why am I afraid of this? As soon as you discover why you were afraid, you are free of this fear and you can let it go. In this way, you make progress. And I still make progress every day.

I remember the movie 'Highlander' with Sean Connery and Christopher Lambert. They were immortal, and yet fighting together for centuries until one of them would remain. And there would be a prize for the winner, but nobody knew what is was. I felt like that; I had been fighting with myself for years and the prize was freedom.

I am confident now, I know myself by heart and I know exactly what I need.
I need to be close to nature, for instance, nature is everything to me. Close to the trees, the animals, the sand and the sea. I live in the South of France to make that possible. To work intensely and energetically, I need to be close to nature.

I was born to be a movie director and producer and I will be like that. And in all my movies the main characters will show this kind of personal work, to become more confident and to become more free, because the answers are not outside, but they are inside yourself.

So I will keep on working every day, to make progress, just like Nadal wants to be better every next day. You have to work on that, to be really free.

And if I can do it, you can do it. It's worth it.

Born in the South of France in 1970, I'm a man of passions. Since my childhood, three passions run in my blood : CINEMA, TV & SPORT. After a University degree in Cinema and Audiovisual, I fulfilled my first dream : to work in the 'Sports on TV' Industry as a Journalist and a Producer. During my 27 years at Canal+Group & Group Tf1, I was in total 100% IMMERSION in the World of Very High Level Sport. And I met Jordan, Kobe, Federer,

Nadal, Bolt, Ronaldo, Zidane...it was a dream come true !
Now, for 2 years, I've been immersed in my second
childhood dream : Cinema.

In other words: my love story has only just begun.

3

BENJAMIN AND WE CALL HIM BEN

By Ailina Boeree

"Applause!"

He often shouted this "cry" after a performance, and it echoed in my head for a long time. With this echo in my head, we performed a last tribute at his coffin.

Benjamin died by suicide on October 24, 2015. He jumped before a train. He was 25 years old.

I was asked: "Do you want to write a story about the impact of suicide on the next of kin?" After looking at a white screen for a long time, and with no idea where to start, a friend sends a text message: October 24, 2020, at 22.40, a documentary film about children who have lost someone to suicide ...

"What else do you want to tell me Ben?"

That night

On October 24, 2015, at 10:40 pm, I was in our cozy caravan with my daughter watching the movie; "As It Is in Heaven", one of Ben's favorite films. Coincidence?

October 24, at 11 pm, I saw a selfie of him on Facebook with the text;"1 love you. Bye." I saw some crazy reactions coming ... "Yes you too bye, bye." I kept looking at this picture, and my abdomen started to hurt. My daughter said he was probably drunk, because he had been to Utrecht with friends that day for a festival. Yes, of course, I wanted to believe that so badly, but my gut kept hurting. After half an hour, I couldn't stand it anymore, I had to be sure.

I texted him;" Hey .. have a question?" I have never received an answer to this app. I texted his colleagues and friends; "where's Ben? I don't know ..."

I called his mother: "Where is Benjamin?", "Ah, sorry, I was sleeping ... no idea."

I called the police at the place where he took that selfie, and told about my gut feeling, and showed them the selfie.

"Yes ma'am, we just got another call from another colleague. We're going to check."

Around midnight, the police called ... I heard a mother's heart cry deep in the distance ... I heard the police-officer breathing heavily through the phone ... I heard the sirens. I knew enough.

My EMDR therapist asked me 2 years later ... "What grade are you giving it now?"

Therapy

Now, 5 years later (we are in 2020), tears still stream down my cheeks. This will never end. Yes, I have now picked up my life again. I am doing well, but this will always remain an open wound, which, I think, I will always have to be carefully disinfect, kept clean, and taken care of.

Many times, the "movie" of the night of October 24, 2015 has passed in my head. My own daughter had a hard time with me. If she didn't text me back, I panicked completely. My work as a theater maker, a trainer for young people in education, was endangered. I saw every kid, including my own daughter, jump in front of the train.

I've tried various forms of therapy, from constellation work to grief therapy. What really helped me is the EMDR. This therapy has brought me to the point that I will not forget it, but that it has become less raw, the sharp edges have been removed.

With EMDR, you tell the moment, with headphones on, what touched you the most, at the same time you hear 'tap, tap, tap' from one ear to the other. Don't ask me why, but it seems to have something to do with the left and right hemispheres of the brain. In this way, trauma can be experienced less violently.

Theatre

Does suicide have an impact on the next of kin? Yes!

I have no judgment about suicide. Who am I to say, whether someone really doesn't want to, or need to, live life anymore?, But that's not what this story is about. The impact is overwhelming.

Benjamin was 16 years old when I first met him. He was in a class that I had to teach. He was a 'wide-smiling' boy with a lot of humor who loved my profession. I was a theatre teacher at an MBO school. It was a wonderful, crazy, playful profession, in which we often went "out of the comfort zone". Because I had been interested in the psyche of man all my life, I had mainly chosen to use theater as a means. Use theater as a means to, for example, make life themes negotiable with young people. That worked very well. In addition to my teaching job, I had an educational theatre company, and our first performance, in collaboration with a crematorium, wanted to make the heavy theme of mourning a little lighter and discussable, and normalize it among young people. Benjamin was very interested in what I was doing from the start. He wanted to do an internship with me, and so be it!

From that day on, he never left my company. This work was also completely in his blood.

Have I been through a lot with him? Yes.

Like many people, there is often a story behind the smile ... Benjamin was no exception.

One of the reasons why I started my company is the focus regarding the waterline in the Netherlands – emphasis is nearly always above the waterline. Education, companies, etc. are mainly focused on visible behavior.

Performance

When I was still working in education as a theatre teacher,

that always surprised me. During my classes, I also noticed how many young people had to work hard to meet the many performance requirements, and how they tried to survive. I often saw adults working hard for these achievements, not only young people. Vulnerability was taboo.

Themes concerning vulnerability, such as grief, were often experienced as difficult and fearful, and when I touched on it in my class, tears came, and I often felt a deep longing in people. There is a desire to be able to share, to flow, even if below the waterline. So, I was very motivated to write and make a performance about it. The first performance 'Rouw op je Dak' was in collaboration with the mourning experts, Riet Fiddelears and Marieke de Bruijn, and presented in Groningen at the Yarden crematorium.

It became a 'hit', and then a company was built around this performance. This was followed by a performance about suicide and depression. A true story of a boy who had taken his own life, who wanted his story to live on in this performance.

These performances are still performed at many schools and care institutions throughout the Netherlands. And every time a string is touched below the waterline and I see time after time the recognition and the desire in young and old to share it.

Benjamin was good at this job. He had completed his internship, and was eager to stay as an actor and trainer. The way I try to deal with all my players is that they feel seen and heard as human beings. But, I had a soft spot for Benjamin. Partly because he was very motivated to grow as an actor and trainer, I developed a personal bond with him. He was a child at home, and my daughter even started to see him as a kind of big brother.
I sensed he felt safe with me, because he could cry, and share some things about his sadness.

Guilt

After his death, I often replayed his stories in my head. What have I missed, what have I not seen, why have I this, and why have I not ...?

Many feelings of guilt have passed. This boy was in a show that was about depression ... this boy played a character with pent-up grief in a show, which could almost have been about him. Why hadn't I seen that properly?

" That's bullshit", friends and family said. But, I had it on my shoulders for a long time --until some grief and suicide experts took me aside, and convinced me that it was his choice. His choice!

My words at his cremation; "It was as if Benjamin had an old soul who, in his short years of life, was able to reach many young hearts through this work. He could hit deep chords like no other, and really see people."

This was also reflected in the cremation ceremony... so many affected people ... I was touched ... touched by all colleagues who had ever worked or still worked for this company ... they were all there.

Benjamin had once said, as a joke to a colleague, if I die, I would like you to sing a song "Welcome to My Head".

I'll never know if it was a joke. To what extent was he engaged with this ... to what extent was it a conscious or an impulsive action? Yes Benjamin was sometimes gloomy and angry with the whole world, but he also had so much humor and zest for life. I never thought he would do this.

Welcome to My Head
You walk in and out, every now and then;
I don't,
I have to stay in my head

Applause

His colleagues took turns getting up, during his cremation ceremony, .. and singing ... Welcome to My Head ... we walked to his coffin .. defeated colleagues hand and hand together ... you walk in and out ... in a large circle we stood around his coffin ... not me, I have to stay in my head ... it became quiet, very quiet ... and a deep bow followed in silence ... a bow to this 25-year-old boy. This boy who had become so dear to me ... a child at home ... this boy with whom I worked so much ... who had become my right hand ... to whom I said "See you tomorrow." almost every day. There would be no "Until tomorrow." ... never again!

Why does one work, and the other not? Does one have a gene, and the other doesn't? We will never understand ... what a lonely battle this must be ... the tears are rising again ... how lonely!

After his death, I no longer had the courage to continue this work. But, because of the many reactions from schools as to whether we wanted to continue with this work, and from several young people that Benjamin had really helped them, we, to this day, continue to play in many schools.

He wanted this so!

Now 5 years later ... the EMDR has taken the edge off ... I was able to continue the company, because I could feel in every cell in my body that he wanted this so. It was also his life's work. Despite his own pain, grief, impotence, he has reached many young hearts ... left love behind ... He will never be forgotten. Now, I can sometimes feel that he might have had to meet me in order to pass on his message of hope and love, even if he had to make a different choice.

It's okay .... Thanks, dear Ben ... how I laughed with you ... you were one of the few who could make me laugh to tears.

Applause for you !!

My name is Ailina Boeree and I founded the TRAXX Foundation in 2004. I am a theatre maker, theatre teacher and the artistic director of theatre TRAXX.

I completed the psycho-social therapist training, specializing in grief and trauma. I also work in secondary vocational education as a trainer on social safety. I supervise classes (and their teachers) when it is "unsafe".

In short, I have a wonderful and rewarding job.

There is a common thread in all my work, namely how do we really make contact with each other, especially under the surface, and also the "normalization" of all life themes for young and old.

www.theatertraxx.nl

4

FROM SUICIDE TO SUCCESS

By Rob Goddard

In 2010, I was on the 125th floor of the world's tallest building, the Burj Khalifa tower in Dubai, preparing for my death. For months I had searched the internet looking for painless ways to kill myself. I decided on jumping from a great height. I calculated that it would only take me 13 seconds to fall nearly 3,000 feet. Then it would all be over. It could be even sooner than that as I had read that I was likely to have a heart attack on the way down. No more pain, nor struggling, just nothing.

Just two years earlier, I was in the top 1% of earners in the

UK. I was 45 years old and in the prime of my life. I had a lovely home, wife and twin boys, and I was highly successful in business. I felt invincible in life, like I was made of granite rock.

However, in a 3-month period in the summer of 2008, my life crumbled. I lost my marriage, my children and my job. I went into an emotional tailspin. I fell out of the sky like an eagle that had been shot by an unknown sniper from the ground. I had never been out of work in my life and as a result I felt like a complete failure in life because I couldn't provide for my family. The centre of my world had been my career and the materialism that surrounded it. I was in a complete state of shock and bewilderment.

Extreme anxiety set in which led me to stop sleeping or eating at all, for days. My mind was in perpetual turmoil trying to process what had happened and how I could sort the whole mess out. I would stare at the TV screen for long periods and not remember what I had just watched. The only thing that filled my waking and non-waking hours was the constant, torturous churn of my disastrous situation.

The day I lost my job I went to see my doctor to get some

medication to help me get through this shock. In her office, I broke down. In floods of tears and broken sentences I managed to get out that I had come to the end of my life and didn't know where to turn. She was empathetic and promised that a counselling service would contact me. Then she handed me a bewildering and colourful array of pills. I thought to myself, "Once the drugs take effect, I'll be back to my normal self within a couple of weeks and then I can start to rebuild my life again".

The Battle

I didn't know that what lay ahead of me was a 5-year battle with depression and me repeatedly feeling that suicide was the only way out. Fortunately, I did meet an "angel" and I'd like to introduce you to him later.

My situational depression was like a black menacing cloud. It came and went as it wanted for many years, affecting my emotions and my mind. I didn't talk to anyone about it, I was too ashamed of feeling the way I did. So, I just put on a brave face, a mask, to the outside world. Contrary to what you may think, it's not suicide that kills, it's the loneliness and isolation. Here's the dichotomy, in a highly connected modern world, we can isolate ourselves so easily. Most depressed people don't want to be a burden on others. Instead, they just suffer in silence and some, sadly, in desperation take their life.

Did you know that 2,200 people a day commit suicide every year on this planet? That's up 40% over the past two decades! Of those, 75% are men. Many men are far worse at expressing their feelings than women. We often lock things away, don't speak up and sometimes the dam breaks. We have a global crisis on our hands. Suicide is the biggest killer of people aged under 45 in the UK. I would have been one of those statistics had events not gone a different route.

By 2010 my life hadn't bounced back, I was still being prescribed drugs by the doctor, but by then I had started to self-medicate with alcohol. Vodka was a quick way of making my mind go fuzzy for a few hours so that I could forget my depression, albeit temporarily. Eventually I stopped taking the prescribed drugs and started stockpiling them instead. In the end I had over 700 pills tucked away in my wardrobe, a secret stash. I thought that if I couldn't control what happened in my life anymore, at least I could determine when and how my life ended. At least I had that control remaining in my life.

Because of regular anxiety attacks, I had numerous restless nights, tossing and turning like a ship caught at sea in an unforgiving storm. I started waking up later, I would keep my dressing gown on throughout the day. I didn't eat properly, didn't shave, and rarely washed. I must have stunk! I had become a functioning alcoholic.

Self-employment was forced upon me, I had no choice. I did manage to slowly build a small business, but it was very tough. I remember travelling to sales pitch meetings with music blaring out of the car's speakers, crying my eyes out en-route, only to discreetly park around the corner from the offices, wipe my eyes and my nose, then put on a mask. I also had a stash of mints in the car to mask the smell of vodka, which I popped before entering the building. I became an "actor" for a couple of hours.

But life just bumped along the bottom, I was just surviving and definitely not thriving. Then, out of the blue my main client terminated our contract and my life again spun immediately out of control. Once again I looked at the dark abyss opening up in front of me.

A Fresh Start

So, in March 2010, I decided to run away to the bright and alluring lights of Dubai to become a Financial Adviser, with the invitation to a job that would provide untold riches for me, or so they promised. In reality, it was a commission only job, working in a part of the world I have never been to and in a culture which I had never encountered previously. It was an opportunity to prove to myself once again that I could bounce back. I had worked in Financial Services for three decades, I believed I could really do it, again.

Initially, I was so full of energy, enthusiasm and renewed hope when I went to see my new Regional Director, at the glitzy Dubai Marina. He was half my age but had been in the country for 4 years and was the top salesman in the company, he had a boat in the Marina and a Porsche 911. At last, a blank canvas, a fresh start where nobody knew me. It may have been commission only and living in one of the most expensive cities in the world, but I was up for the challenge.

I started my new job with no data, no client base, no website, no marketing budget, just me and a bunch of business cards and a winning smile! I figured that my target market included expatriates, high net worth individuals who paid no tax and were dripping with surplus cash. So, I decided to go where they tend to hang out, meet them, chat and make myself visible. Places like the Yacht Marina, the Irish pub Fibber's McGee, The Polo Club and the prestigious car dealerships like Ferrari, Lamborghini, Porsche, even the Harley Davidson dealership. I also used LinkedIn, creating a stream of articles on "hot topics" of interest to some of the worlds' richest people, positioning myself as a "thought leader" in all matters financial. Leads started to flood in, new clients were signing up and at last I was making some serious money again.

However, I had completely underestimated trying to fit in with an immensely fast-moving society and, what seemed to me at least, was a superficial and uncaring environment. A micro climate where people rarely had the time or inclination to build real friendships. At the same time, I had also cut myself off from my family and my close friends, working in a country 3,500 miles away.

The blazing summer sun was like an inferno and coupled with the stifling humidity of Dubai, it was like working in my own hell. I felt like a prisoner condemned to a life of hard labour, paying for my heinous crimes. The money wasn't bringing happiness at all, I was gradually feeling alone in the metropolis. Isolated from family and close friends. It was a prison of my own making, albeit a golden one.

The End

I gradually sunk into what felt like quicksand. The more I struggled against it, the more I got sucked into it. So, I kept what I called a "death diary." It was me journaling about my innermost thoughts, fears and anxieties. It helped to write things down, but the main aim was to leave something behind for my children, so that they would know why their Dad had killed himself. I didn't want them to blame themselves or think they could have done something to change the situation.

After months of battling on my own, I eventually gave up the fight. I was emotionally exhausted and battle weary, so I decided to go to the daunting and imposing tower of the Burj Khalifa, to find my way outside to jump. 13 seconds away from ending the pain and private hell that had become my life.

I woke up one morning and decided that today would be the day this torment would end. I showered and shaved like any normal day. I then phoned a work colleague and said that I wanted to visit the Burj Khalifa and take some pictures from the top of the tower, because despite working in Dubai, I never had time to do the tourist thing. I never disclosed to him my plan because I didn't want him to talk me out of it.

I met him at the front entrance, bought the tickets and joined the snaking queue of sightseers making their way to the lifts. As we travelled the 90 seconds to the top I recall having this macabre thought that it would only take me 13 seconds to come back down. I was calm, not stressing about what I was about to do. A It was a surreal frame of mind to be in, having made the decision to end my pain. I felt empowered somehow to be taking control of my life.

We got to the 125th floor and wandered around the viewing platform with a multitude of tourists. I asked my friend to take some pictures of me looking out at the Dubai scenery and then excused myself to the bathroom. I told him I wouldn't be long. Instead, I went around the tower looking for a way to the outside of the building. The viewing platforms are floor to ceiling thick glass, so I had to find an exit that workers use to gain access to the outside of the tower.

I quickly found a fire exit and tentatively tried the handle. It was locked! Who on earth locks a fire exit door? This one was and so my attempt at suicide that day had been thwarted. I went back to my apartment, dejected, miserable and angry with myself. The stock pile of 700+ tablets looked more appealing.

A call for help

I'm not sure why, but I decided to call a friend of mine back in the UK. Alex and I had met at a business networking event just at the time I had first gone self-employed. There was an immediate connection between us and over a couple of years we became good friends. He was and still is a Business Coach and crucially, he was the only person who kept in regular contact with me after I left for Dubai. He contacted me on a regular basis to see how things were going. I looked forward to our chats. Although,

I didn't really share the full picture, I just tried to be upbeat.

But, following my thwarted suicide attempt earlier that day, I offered to fly him out to Dubai for a few days, so that we could speak in person and at length. To my surprise he jumped on a plane and we sat poolside at my apartment for hours on end. We also laughed incessantly. It was fun sharing time together. He also told me off when he peered in my fridge and challenged me with *"I can't see anything green, only meat and alcohol!"*

Alex asked me one question that changed the direction of my life. He asked, *"What do you **really** want to do with your life Rob?"* Immediately, I said that I didn't know. But not put off by that, he persisted with, *"but if you did know, what would it look like?"*

What a great question. I then began to describe what I saw and said that I wanted to go back to my first love of Mergers and Acquisitions. With more prodding, visualizing and planning a potentially happy future, I subsequently made the decision to return back to the UK to start again.

A new life

I went on to envisage that by 2020 I would create a
business worth £5m+, move somewhere in the Southern
Mediterranean and I would teach English to children from a
double-decker bus, and with the woman of my dreams.

With renewed hope and a clearer vision, I managed to pitch
and secure 14 investors for my new business venture. I was
then able to afford to pay myself a salary for the first time
in 3 years. It's not been easy building a business from
nothing, but with unwavering determination, that fledgling
business has now grown into a multi-million-pound
company across two continents, employing 25 people.

Nevertheless, I still had to kill a few ghosts from the past,
so 3 years ago I set up a sister company in Dubai. The first
time round in Dubai I was a beaten man, now when I come
out of the airport terminal, I have a smile back on my face
in a country that so nearly became my last resting place.
Initially, I was apprehensive and unsure if I could make a
business work out there, having failed previously.
However, I felt much stronger than before. Because the UK
business had some success, I used that as my confidence
platform for the new Dubai business.

Over the years I have learnt from my mistakes of the past and have surrounded myself with trusted people that I can share myself with, people who act as sounding board, both in business and on a personal level. I've also set out to employ people better than me at things. There is a freedom in having others run the business day to day. That enabled me to have precious time back and I now own 4 businesses and don't work full time in any of them!

Retirement has allowed me to do the things I want with the people that I want to work with. I've broken the walls of that golden prison and have been teaching clients to do the same for the past 10 years. I now help business owners find an exit strategy, closing one chapter in their life and starting a new one. That's been my journey and I want to share with others how liberating that is. I also invest in other people's businesses and take on a few private clients for mentoring assignments. I have the privilege of being asked to speak at a wide range of other people's events, both in the UK and in the Gulf.

The Road Forward

Looking back, my resilience, the strength I found to fight

back and triumph over adversity, came from speaking and sharing with others. Today I know there's no point in running away. Even in the darkest hour, it's healthier to just face-up and reach out in dark times.

My relationship with money has changed too. In fact, I'm in the process of setting up a charity in order to embark on a 10-year plan to create a "living legacy." An altruistic journey to make a difference to other people's lives, through a multitude of charitable causes to those in need.

My family has expanded, I now have 6 children ranging from the ages of 25 down to 6, with two sets of twins in that beautiful tribe! Had I been successful in my suicide attempt, I would have robbed all of them of a future with their Father.

I would also never have gotten together with Kristina, the woman of my dreams, either. She is originally from Albania and we have a 2nd home there on the beach overlooking the Mediterranean Sea. We've bought boat too and still plan to buy that Double Decker bus soon.

Retirement to me is being able to do the things I choose to

do, with the people that I want to be with. I can't wait for the next 10-year vision to unfold, building a charitable foundation, with the woman of my dreams, and experiencing the joy of making a difference in life.

Find an Alex

One final thought. If you are struggling right now and if you are in a dark, cold place, I urge you to find an "Alex".

Specifically;

- Speak up and ask for help. You will **not** be a burden on anyone. Don't let isolation win. Make that call now to a trusted person. They will be honoured that you have shared something so personal with them and that you trust them.

- Don't believe the lie in your head that the world would be a better place without you in it. Dozens of people will be devastated by you taking your own life and that will affect them for the rest of their lives. Suicide is a long-term solution to a short-term problem.

Alternatively, if life is ok for you, consider becoming an "Alex" to someone that you suspect is going through a hard time. Go for a coffee or lunch and give them time and space to open up. Let them know you are there for them, any time, any place. Give them your listening ear, not instant fixes. You could be that one person they need to help turn things around. There is no better feeling to know that you have been instrumental in saving someone's life, just ask my friend, Alex.

Rob now owns four businesses and has transitioned from an operator to investor - a journey many entrepreneurs struggle to make. He has trained over 6,000 business leaders and brings over 35 years experience of helping business owners finish one chapter in their lives and start a new one.

His original and largest business, EvolutionCBS Ltd is a highly successful multi-million pound advisory firm in the UK and UAE, and since 2002 Rob has been responsible for the sale of nearly 400 privately-owned UK businesses, totaling over £2 billion in transaction values.

Rob also works on more philanthropic and altruistic projects and causes, especially in the area of depression and suicide. His signature talk, "Suicide to Success," is a very personal story of his own battle with depression, leading to a suicide attempt, then fighting back to win and triumph over adversity, to lead a fulfilling life, filled with fun.

Website: www.robgoddard.co.uk
Email: rob.goddard@robgoddard.co.uk
LinkedIn: linkedin.com/in/robgoddard
Amazon Book:
        https://www.amazon.co.uk/dp/1916220401/ref=rdr_ext_tmb

5

LET GO OF YOUR BELIEFS AND TRANSFORM YOURSELF

By Yvonne Lorang

It's totally unimaginable that someone you love can be suddenly ripped from life.
It's unimaginable that someone you love chooses to leave his or her own life.

It's even more unimaginable that someone is doing so without telling anyone and so doing it all alone. That is not only painfully lonely, that is the saddest thing I've ever heard. When this happens to someone you love deeply it leaves a big wound in your heart.

This unimaginable, painful and irreversible choice was made by my brother in 2013. Although I didn't understand his choice at that time, I do understand now.

October 2012

My phone rings.

'Hey what's up brother?'

'Hey sis. What are you doing?'

'I just walked out of my office and I am walking to my car. I made a lot of soap today but it's late, I'm cold and I'm hungry so I should hurry to buy some food before the supermarket closes. As usual I haven't prepared anything. Why?'

'I think I start to understand how that must feel. I never realized how hard that must be for you. Coming home alone, no one waiting for you or to eat dinner with. Or to come home after a holiday and find an empty fridge waiting for you. All those things. I just never thought about it till today. And the worst thing about it is that I never questioned this myself. I never asked myself if my little sister is strong or not. If you enjoy being alone or not. To me you appear strong, but are you?'

'It's not a matter of being strong or not. I don't have a choice. I don't think I can be as strong as you'.

'You know, I'm sitting in my car on the parking lot at the Amsterdam Arena to attend a big VIP evening in the VIP box first row and I'm an hour too early. Besides that, I totally don't feel like going.'

'You sound strange. Why are you sitting in your car on an empty parking lot an hour before you should be there?'

'I don't know sis...'

Typically my brother, never opening up about his feelings. Well, at least not towards me.
And when I tried to be open with him in the past he always talked about other stuff, like he really didn't want to go down that road. Also hugging was difficult for him. Each time I tried to get a real hug from him he did hug me but he couldn't hold me the way I longed for. He would hold me, but instead of wrapping his arms around me he would pat my back.

His job was what he loved the most, well not after his kids were born of course, but he loved it and it didn't appear to be work. In my eyes he was always doing fun stuff. Events, dinners, playing golf and in the meantime he was making big sales-deals. Everybody liked him, because of his natural charm and that made his job easy.

He was very inventive too. He knew how to design the right package for the right product in such a way that a customer would buy the product only because of it's appearance and how it was presented. The big brands in the food industry were benefiting from his talents and business related "friends" often advised him to start his own company. But my brother liked financial security.

'You know what? She wants a divorce. '

I was speechless. Nineteen years of marriage and together for twenty tree years is a lot to end just like that but she must have had a good reason, I hoped.

'Apparently it's my time to be in deep shit and you know all about it!
And while I'm saying this I suddenly realize that I've never been there for you during all of these difficult moments you had to encounter in your life. I am so sorry for that!'

For the first time he sounded warm and vulnerable and his voice was shaky. And although I felt the urge to respond with a soft voice I couldn't. Not because of this announcement of his divorce but because of his apologies. I couldn't respond because it was true. He had never been there for me when I needed him the most.

And now he sounded so warm and so close. It made me smile internally but at the same time I felt terrible because he sounded so broken. From that moment on, something crucial changed in the bond we had.

I advised him to go to the event and find himself some distraction. And I suggested we would call the day after. I also urged him to call me whenever he needed me, no matter what time of the day.

'That sounds very nice sis, I might make use of it. '

I realized where the emotional detachment came from. This was due to our past and the fact that we were separated from each other at a young age.

Separation

My siblings were born during our mother's first marriage but unfortunately this ended in a divorce. My mother remarried and soon I was born. When I was tree years old we moved, as a family, to the South of France but without my brother! He stayed behind in the Netherlands to live with *his* father, a choice in which he had no say. We only saw our brother during school holidays.

After a few years the marriage between my parents came to an end as well. My mother and sister stayed in France, my brother was already living with *his* father and I went back to Holland to live with *my* father. This is how we were torn apart between our parents.

Our mother turned out to be ill and when I was nine, my sister and brother respectively thirteen and sixteen, our mother died due to breast cancer.

No one told me the truth about her illness and even worse, it was my mother's wish that I would not go to her funeral because she thought I was too young. Actually, it was the worst thing she could do. Children need openness. I needed openness when I was a kid but I didn't get it. It therefore took me many years to understand my youth and to be able to really grieve for the loss. But our mother's death also had another profound impact on us. Like my brother I had also shut down emotionally and deep down this had its consequences. All three of us missed a mother, a secure environment to grow up in. It was all violated.

My youth had a tremendous effect on my life. On all of us.

At the age of twenty-six I was diagnosed with breast cancer myself. I had just bought my first house and was facing a rough time ahead. That was when I needed my family the most but during that period my brother hardly showed up. I managed to get my life back on track. It wasn't easy because I had lost trust in my body and in life but little by little, as the years passed, I overcame everything. Seven years later, during a routine check, I was diagnosed again and I lost the last bit of confidence.

To my own surprise I seemed to be stronger than I thought. It was again a rough time with a lot of hospital visits but during the months of recovery I decided not to wait any longer and to start doing what I really wanted to do: a long trip around the world. And so I did. I sold my house, I left my job and started traveling. Funny enough I had more contact with my brother when I was on the other side of the globe. Why didn't we had this kind of contact when I was at home and when I was ill? I stopped asking myself and just enjoyed it for as long as it could because I learned to live in the moment. I just couldn't look into the future any longer.

One and a half year later I returned to Holland. To my father, my siblings and my friends. In the first year I took a job opportunity at the International Criminal Tribunal for the Former Yugoslavia. Although I didn't spend all my money, the job was needed to get my financial situation back on track in order to pay a reasonable rent for my first apartment.

After that I started my own company. While traveling a creative side was sparked in me and so after work, in my spare time, I started to make soap. This hobby got out of hand and before I knew it I had this beautiful soap brand in hands. But then you still have to sell it and so I asked my brother for advice.

October 2013

My phone rings.

I received a pleasant phone-call. The result of something I had worked so hard for lately. One the biggest perfume-stores of The Netherlands wanted to place an order.

I had invested all my money into this soap brand so this was a fantastic chance. I was so happy and delighted and so was my brother - but his voice betrayed him.

Since that phone call in October 2012 my brother and I stayed connected daily. He became absolutely more honest about his feelings too.

But when a few months later his wife moved out he was really losing himself. In the meantime he had lost his job as well and that started to make him feel unworthy. He said that he felt useless.

We started to worry to an extent that we asked him to see his general practitioner and he immediately sent our brother to a psychiatrist.

One day I received a phone call from one of his *work* related friends. A total stranger to me. He told me that my brother called him daily and made him promise to keep their phone calls private but he could no longer keep this promise.

The weight on his shoulders became too heavy he said. My brother seemed to deal with suicidal thoughts. I was shocked.

This is when we really started to get worried but my sister and I couldn't tell our brother about this phone call. He also had told this friend that his kids would be better off without him. We did everything we could. During the whole summer we tried to support him where ever we could. My sister assisted him with practical stuff as she was good in organizing things. I lived closer to my brother and helped him with some cooking, reading bedtime stories to my nephews and taking him to the beach for a walk.

I also accompanied him to several appointments with the psychiatrist.

Early November I was at my computer to reply to some emails when I received a long email from my brother. I went through it in no time and I felt my stomach turn and I immediately knew something was seriously wrong. Intuitively and rapidly I scrolled to the end of the email and read what I was already afraid of…

Dear sisters,
I love you unconditionally...

October 2020

Seven years without my brother.
The reason I wrote down my story is because it's absolutely necessary.

I might have known how he felt the day he committed suicide because sixteen months after my brother's death I shortly stood – for a split second - in his footsteps.

The day my life came to a complete standstill.

The day I might have understood my brother's choice.

I chose to step away from that place.

A turning point? Absolutely!

My brother left a big wound in my heart and a hole in my soul. The next two years were difficult but I had had some experience with difficulty. I had to necessarily let go of my past and invest time and energy into my future. I had to clean my past, to let go of my beliefs and to completely transform myself. I had to learn to love myself. The love my brother and I may have missed due to the loss of our mother.

And when I was done with all that I bumped into one of my brother's oldest best friend and we fell in love with each other.

With my contribution to this book I would like to encourage all people with similar lives, problems or thoughts to heal themselves. Use this story as an example.

You can do it.

STEPHANIE VAN DER WIEL PHOTOGRAPHY

Late 2014 Yvonne's life came to a complete standstill. She was 43 and she experienced the consequences of living in a survival mode that could no longer be sustained. Not physically, not emotionally and not financially. She had touched rock bottom and there was only one way to go: *UP!*

A turning point in which she unexpectedly discovered an inner strength that helped her to find her way back to life. She started to ask questions. To the universe or to whoever was listening: *"Why am I so strong?"* & *"Why did I survive all of these setbacks?"*

Her remarkable capacity for resilience stands out compared to others and this gave her the idea to help people to discover their own strength in the most difficult time of their lives.

With her drive and hunger for knowledge she became a life coach, a therapist, an author and a public speaker. She combines her practice with lectures throughout the country to share her story and her experiences.

"With warm feelings from the deepest of her heart she greets you and asks you to never ever give up".

6

SUICIDE: A DEADLY THOUGHT?

By Paul Lowe

In your life, have you ever stopped to ask yourself why emotionally, you felt so strongly about taking a certain course of action – whether deemed major or minor – even when mentally, it made very little sense to do so?

Isn't it true that most of us at some time or other, when we've come to a crossroads, will have experienced extremely confusing thoughts – irrespective of the perceived size of the dilemma faced – that left us feeling uncertain and insecure?

Isn't it also true that generally as human beings, we rely

heavily on our need for certainty, and if that is not being met for whatever reason, fear is allowed to creep in and start to bully our mind?

So what drives me to write this particular chapter, for this much-needed book?

The answer is very simple: to share my own suicide-related experiences in the hope that readers' **Awareness** may be raised, **Beliefs** may be challenged and ultimately, better **Choices** may result. Interestingly, what do the first letters of these three vitally meaningful words spell? ABC.

As a child, what's one of the first things we ever learn – the alphabet, right? Maybe there is more than a little significance in this; something we will re-visit, later...

A Child Without Love Or Hope

Let's continue by asking a fairly controversial question: Why should we take care of and love children in general? Perhaps a plausible response is encompassed within some lyrics from the well-known *Greatest Love Of All* song – 'I believe that children are our future.'

Taking this a stage further: why should you care for your own children? Surely the answer dramatically starts to get more heart-felt now, and cannot be addressed by simply quoting a line from a best-selling song?

How about we really focus in now, and imagine you only had one child, and you had abused that beautiful soul so much, that (s)he became a totally defenseless, isolated, and vulnerable being?

As an only child, that's exactly what started to happen to me. My pain and suffering started way-back in 1968 as a boy of eight—when my mother re-married. That marriage brought into our home a man who subsequently subjected mother and child to tortuous escalating acts of emotional abuse, wanton neglect, mental cruelty, and ultimately terrible physical violence. Despite countless promises to change, the situation consistently worsened. So much so that I gave him the label of 'The Beast'.

Picture your life as a puzzle, and with the passing of time, you fit more and more pieces together to complete the picture – like a jigsaw. The Beast was a monster piece in my puzzle. As much as I vaguely remembered the first eight years of my life with pride and happiness – a nostalgic golden era of my passions for music and football – I'm equally polarised in my **Awareness** of how The Beast destructively changed my life.

My only salvation through that living hell were the rock-solid **Beliefs** that one day, I would be playing professional football for my hometown club, Nottingham Forest. But even that dream was facing a new challenge...my mother was a secret drinker and by the age of 12, I became addicted to her stashes of sherry and whisky.

That day

I guess when we each look back on our often-uncertain journey, one certainty is that we all have **Choices** to make. Within those choices, there may be at least one life-defining moment; a turning point that contributed significantly – for better or worse – to the subsequent path we then took.

One such turning point for me, goes way back to Saturday 23rd March 1974 when – at the tender age of 13½ – I could not cope any more, and decided the only way to stop my hell-on-earth would be to end my life.

Armed with a razor blade, I managed to escape from my 'prison' (bedroom) and run away to the solitude of the nearby 'Dicky-Dydows'– a derelict, secluded area where the old coal trains used to pass through.

Obviously – by the mere fact I'm able to pen this chapter –
I didn't succeed. So enter that all-important question again:
'Why?'

This is the first time I have ever shared in writing what
actually happened on that fateful Saturday evening, and I
honestly don't know why that is. Maybe subconsciously I
believed to share the details of the experience would seem
so 'far out there' to others, and they would judge me, think
I'm crazy, or even stop loving me. This whole fear-based
thinking is the undoubted power of our deep-rooted
subconscious.

So what did happen?

As I sat back against a small cave wall – totally alone and
frightened – I remember holding the razor in my right hand,
knowing one swipe across my left wrist and all the misery
would be over. But something beyond profound
happened…I felt a powerful push from behind, despite
being sat against a wall, and I fell forward with unstoppable
force. Something literally pushed me out of a dark place!

A couple more equally profound unexplainable things
happened too – I broke down and cried incessantly,

something I hadn't done for years (being conditioned by The Beast, that 'big boys don't cry'). Also, after I managed to stem the floods of tears, I couldn't find the razor – it had disappeared!

People often talk about fight-or-flight, and I suppose what I understood in a very basic way – within that life-defining moment – was that I would never flee again, and from that point onwards, I would only ever fight.

As the years have gone by, I have been able to make sense of something which, at the time, I had neither the emotional nor intellectual capacity to comprehend. All I came to understand from those unexplainable experiences was that my purpose in life would be to fight for those that couldn't fight for themselves – I had become a rebel WITH a cause.

Despite this new-found purpose, my world was in complete turmoil, and I felt like a child without love or hope...

Unbearable Growing Pains

Although I was naturally a loving, caring, and sensitive type of child, I had found myself developing a safety mechanism that kept people at arm's length: namely, acting aggressive and confrontational, even when I didn't feel that way in reality. In effect, I was living a massive lie.

Consequently, in November 1974, things were about to come to a head and change forever. After being kept behind at school for a detention, I knew that returning home late that afternoon would mean big trouble, although The Beast never needed a reason. Being on the end of his violent and abusive attacks were a part of 'normal' life for my mother and me.

I began trembling with anticipation before sprinting towards home, with all the adrenaline and nervous energy of a hunted gazelle. As I entered the back door, the inevitable happened.

The Beast attacked me incessantly. I somehow weathered the onslaught and wiped the streams of crimson blood from my face.

As I did so, I managed to catch sight of a bread knife on the kitchen table. I lunged for it and took my stance with only one thought in mind, and it wasn't to cut bread! The hunted had now become the hunter, and my temper was so fierce, like a caged and tormented tiger.

The winds of change were blowing, and this was the first time I became conscious of my ability to take back control of my life away from The Beast. Like all bullies when threatened with their own treatment, he cowered and backed off.

The anticipated violent sequel having not materialized, my mother and I simply packed our bags and left, with yours truly vowing to The Beast that one day I would return and get my revenge.

A Rebel with a Cause

This proved to be a significant turning point in my life. Because of all the emotional pain I had suffered over the previous few years, I now found myself more than ever becoming alcohol dependent, whilst at the same time, becoming embroiled in constant conflict and fights.

As I progressed beyond my teens, one of the lowest points of my life occurred on New Year's Eve 1982, with the news that my grandma Winnie had died. As an 'old-school' matriarch, she was so resilient, strong, and was as solid and tough as a majestic oak tree.

After Winnie's death, to say I waged war on society would be a massive understatement. I took it upon myself to be judge, jury, and executioner towards any Tom, Dick, or Harry that I perceived was a bully. My self-identity of being a rebel with a cause became unshakably strong.

For a while, sheer willpower and determination saw me turn things around. At the age of 23, I got married, and by 27, had two beautiful children and a third on the way. However, the cracks soon re-appeared because I had never managed to consistently curb my alcohol addiction – the demon drink had me firmly in its vice-like clutches.

In June 1988 – some fourteen years on – I reached rock-bottom in my life.

I split up from my wife and kids and began to drift into complete oblivion. Like all heavy drinkers, my thought processes had become badly distorted; thus, I couldn't rid myself of the crippling, destructive memories relating to the previous years of torture and abuse.

It was at this point that I finally confronted The Beast, first physically, and later, in my mind and psyche. All those years of hatred had been allowed to fester and in my emotionally-twisted logic, it was now time to redress the balance for all the anguish, pain and suffering he had caused. For fourteen years, I had constantly re-lived every slap, punch, and sadistic act that The Beast had delivered to my mother and me.

The upshot was I intended to kill him, but whilst I fatefully tried to do my 'duty', the Universe intervened, and my intention was not fulfilled. This meant both our lives were spared – his from death, and mine from serving a life sentence in prison.

Black & White

The reality, though, was my life sentence in prison (my mind) was continuing; in fact, my demons were getting deeper and darker. My mind kept constantly meandering back to that dark and desperate night of Saturday 23 March 1974, with no resolution.

The years went by with my life being an extremely polarized seesaw of black and white experiences. When I was in a 'white phase', I would be off the drink, earning good money, and generally committing to many charitable and community fund-raising events.

Trouble was, I wasn't able to sustain this, and would – within a matter of weeks – revert back to a 'black phase', resulting in prolonged drinking bouts, sometimes months on end. The reality was, I had really deep-rooted psychological issues, underpinned by a self-sabotaging, self-hate. It was like constantly being on a see-saw that fluctuated between embracing spiritual light, and the darkness of physical death.

During these decades of a topsy-turvy existence, I experienced the ultimate highs and lows of life, with neither being consistent. The only certainty I knew was uncertainty! My charitable work gave me significance, though, as well as love and connection.

In 1998, the see-saw dipped toward the black end and nearly stayed there. Suicide raised its grotesque head again, this time relating to a very close friend. The name and details serve no purpose, other than to say for two years, I listened to the individual propound the power of the 'seven-year itch' – believing that bad things come around every seven years.

And so, the self-fulfilling prophecy came true. Seven years after having a nervous breakdown, this beautiful soul I had known since childhood ended it all. For a long time afterwards, my own demons got fuel for their fire through the guilt and remorse of thinking I could have prevented my friend's death.

As a result, I have subsequently spent years researching strategies and techniques – as well as developing my own concepts – around how we may alleviate deadly suicidal thoughts. Undoubtedly, there are so many different perspectives that could be offered in regard this life-preserving challenge, but there is one that unswervingly resonates with me: The power of thought.

Thoughts Change Lives

Of course, there is never a one-size-fits-all solution to life's many and varied challenges, and I certainly wouldn't wish to appear insensitive by offering 'simple' solutions to something as devastating and heart-breaking as suicide.

That said, I know first-hand – from my own experiential learning – how dramatically thoughts can change lives, and as such, I humbly share some insights and thoughts around three broad areas that have helped me make the transformational journey from pain to purpose.

Remember the ABC I alluded to at the beginning? Awareness, Beliefs and Choices have a role to play in re-thinking the way we think about suicide.

Awareness. How many of us are actually aware of our

inner child, let alone the significance it continues to have in our life?

Beliefs. These influence our thoughts, feelings, words, actions and ultimately, the outcome. Learn to believe in yourself.

Choices. The reality is, we all have choices in life, and no matter how seemingly impossible the situation is, there is ALWAYS hope.

Loving

Remember at the beginning of this chapter when I made reference to only having one child, and how that beautiful soul had been abused so much that (s)he became a totally defenceless, isolated, and vulnerable being? I didn't refer to any child I have produced. I refer to the one inside me.

So let's get really specific now, and identify…our Inner Child. Whilst it's fair to say that as a child, I – along with my protective mother – experienced barbaric, horrific treatment at the hands of The Beast, inadvertently I allowed the legacy of this to carry on throughout the biggest part of my adult life. I let myself be consumed by fear, anger, deservedness issues, self-hate, hopelessness, and a near life-long alcohol addiction.

Would you deliberately heap all this dark, destructive misery onto one of your own beloved children? Of course you wouldn't. So why do we continue to ignore that tender inner child, the one that is asking us for love and forgiveness?

Learning to develop a loving relationship with my own inner child has undoubtedly been a key factor in being able to enjoy a life of (inner) peace. Does that mean I don't face life's everyday challenges? Of course not, but surely how we handle those challenges is what really matters.

Legacy

I have come to embrace the power of purpose as an antidote to despair. I firmly believe that each and every one of us is a unique soul with a special gift/ talent to offer the world. As Picasso offered:

The meaning of life is to find your gift;

the purpose of life is to give it away

As we embrace the 'Six Human Needs' model (Robbins), there is immense power in understanding we do everything in life to meet a need, including needs for:

❖ Certainty

❖ Uncertainty

❖ Significance

❖ Love & Connection

❖ Growth

❖ Contribution

Contribution is another word for legacy.

Once again, I humbly share that these days, I constantly strive towards meeting the highest (spiritual) need of Contribution. This manifests itself in the work I do through World Game-Changers – being privileged to serve with a small army of compassionate people – with everyone dedicated to:

Planting The Seeds For Change

Planting those seeds of light is not easy when you may find yourself in the darkest of places, but sometimes with a nudge or push from the Universe, you can be moved to make a different choice. I have come to know the immense power of thoughts, and how choosing self-love thoughts over fear-based alternatives results in a radically more self-empowering outcome.

My final message of love & hope: even life's most beautiful flowers spend time in a dark. earthly place – needing time and nurturing, to bloom…

From an early age, Paul was in the vice-like clutches of the demon drink and constantly embroiled within a dark cocktail of toxic beliefs, self-hate, and destructive violence.

He has made a remarkable transformation from existing for many years in despair; to now living a really healthy, happy, and fulfilling life – spending most of his time in the sunny climes of south-east Spain.

Paul's purpose is deeply transformational…

Developing World Game-Changers

Through his *Mastering The Game Of Life* books and podcasts, he creates the space and platforms for others to be heard. Paul totally understands we all have vital messages to share, and it is part of his mission to assist people's voices to be heard – particularly our young people.

He has a long and distinguished history of heart-centred coaching & mentoring, specializing in enabling others to enjoy a similar life of health, happiness, and fulfilment.

Paul has been responsible for raising very significant amounts of funds for many charities and good causes around the world; moreover, he has positively inspired and uplifted thousands of children – mainly from challenging backgrounds – both within his native UK, and worldwide.

As the founder of World Game-Changers (Community Interest Company), Paul has dedicated decades of his life developing many life-empowering initiatives, all concentrated around *Mastering The Game Of Life.*

www.Paul-Lowe.com

www.WorldGameChangers.org

7

SURVIVING TORN CONNECTIONS

By B.C. Peeters

I was born at the beginning of the 1950s in Flanders, that is in Belgium. I was the middle of the five children. I had two older sisters and after me came another sister and a brother.

My father had a practice next to our house, so he was always close by. I can't remember very many of my early childhood years; I have the feeling that they went quite "normally," as they do for most children. At home we had two "cleaning women" for the household and a live-in child-help who, for example, gave me a bath. I don't really remember if my mother took care of us herself.

Depression

Actually, it was only from my twelfth year that the situation changed drastically. At that age one day I found my mother lying in bed depressed. From that moment on, that depression has largely determined her and our lives, right up to her self-imposed death.

What caused that depression is still a guess for me. I was once diagnosed with "bipolarity," and perhaps she was. But at that time this was hardly known, let alone that there was any attention for it.

For my mom, however, it had everything to do with her relationship. She accused my father of paying too little attention to matters that she considered important. She constantly indicated that she was not happy and she also said at one point, "I feel like a bird in a golden cage." In those years she tried to escape that by being away from home often. She would have gone by bicycle and none of us knew where to go. We would come home from school and Mother would be gone. And when my father came home he asked us where our mother was, but we didn't know that. Thus, as children, we were given a kind of responsibility that was completely out of step with our age.

We, as children, could at one point imagine that my mother would want to divorce my father. My second sister and I even gave her some encouragement and offered to help her. But she didn't want to.

Later I also started to wonder if her story was the right one. It was also conceivable that because of her depression she saw everything in a certain way and that translated into reproaches against my father. And perhaps my father did his very best to deal with my mother's manic moods as best he could. I find that very difficult to interpret and I do not know the answer exactly.

A Death Wish

What I do know is that my father knew about my mother's death wish and that he accepted it at some point. He accepted that she wanted to get out of life. Perhaps after all these years he had also more or less given up.

I never actually talked about this with my father, also because he died of cancer seven years after my mother's death. He had been walking around for several years with a small wound on his arm, which would not heal but for which he did not seek advice or diagnosis. He also developed prostate cancer, which has spread to the brain, among others. Had he given up on life?

Back then, it was in the early 1980s, my mother dropped herself from the curb in the canal after taking a cocktail of medicines and drowned in it. When they found her, she was already dead. I was 29 at the time, my younger sister 26 and my brother 23. My two eldest sisters had left home for years; they have been going to boarding school since they were twelve, and at that time often came home for a weekend only once every two weeks. So they have received these daily conditions much less.

At one point my mother received medication and she took it for years. But we saw that it didn't really help and my older sister and I encouraged her to seek therapy.

Therapy

I myself went into therapy during that time. I noticed that I had problems and had read a lot about it. I was raised a Catholic and Catholicism was prominent in the fathers and mothers families. My father had two brothers who had stepped in, and my mother had a brother and a sister who had also. I had a great imagination as a child and I believed everything I was told about hell and purgatory. I believed that "God was everywhere and knew me in the depths of my mind." That idea was unbearable to me; it robbed me of all my freedom.

My problems grew in the years that I discovered sexuality. I got caught in a compulsive spiral of lust and guilt that kept alternating. That feeling grew stronger when I had a homosexual relationship with a cousin for some time. That relationship ended abruptly - it also turned out that he had a boyfriend - and that was a new traumatic experience for me. I felt like a sinner and was full of guilt. I had so many problems with that that it went badly at school and I ended up in therapy.

In our family, the children talked about the problems of fathers and mothers, but it was never really about feelings. It was usually about who was right, my father or my mother. And there was an internal discussion about this and we never agreed.Such discussions were always kept in private, nothing was said to the outside world.

I remember once, when I was about twenty, saying something to the pastor and to a brother of my father; that it no longer went like this in our house. But that did not help then either.

Living my own life

After a break, I finally finished high school. After that came a number of years of varying study choices and a constant struggle with the demands of the study and my own psychological problems. I was lonely, depressed, and still struggling with my homosexual feelings and fear of it.

Eventually I returned home and went to night school for music. I had been playing the piano since I was twelve and I could put a lot of my feelings into it. After night school I was allowed to go to the conservatory, but I have not managed to do that for more than two years.

Then I went to work. I became a bus driver and from that moment on I lived on my own. I kept that job for a year, but after that I became terrified of the predictability of such a professional life.

Then it became a mixture of periods of unemployment with a job or running a health food store.

I learned about my mother's death from my father and my sister. They came to my door to tell. I remember being very angry with my dad, but I didn't let him know. Little or nothing was said about the death of my mother afterwards.

After the funeral, everyone was happy. There was champagne and no one spoke about my mother. I didn't understand that.

Brother and sister

My youngest brother had a close relationship with my mother. He supported her almost daily and her death caused him much psychological damage. He developed psychosis and had to drop out of his studies. A few months after my mother's death, he made an attempt to take his own life. He hanged himself, but my father found him in time and he survived. My brother never took up his studies again, he was admitted several times and then started working in a form of protected work. We would meet up and then go for a walk, but I have had a few times where he got into a kind of state where he showered me with reproaches, as if I was to blame for everything. I attributed that to his condition, but it was not pleasant to experience.

My younger sister was torn between my father's world and my mother's. For her they were very much separated and she saw no opportunity to bridge them for herself. Or create their own world for themselves. My sister suffered from depression and has also received regular therapy. We just didn't feel that it helped in the least. I had the same with her

94

as with my brother: her mood could change from one moment to the next and then she got angry with me because we sold the business or because of all kinds of other things she blamed us. Eventually my sister got married and from that marriage a daughter was born. But the marriage broke down and my sister saw no opportunity to fulfill the role of mother properly. Her daughter was then placed in foster care and all those sad events were added to the events of her childhood. Then she had another child with another man, but history repeated itself. That child also ended up in a foster family. And my sister could not find a job and could not find her psychological peace with such a past. She ended it then, in a very dramatic way.

One bad day she set herself on fire in the reception hall of a bank and she died from the injuries. The bizarre thing is that she did this in the same year of life (59) as her mother once did. My sister had so much fiery anger that she feared and could not handle. I think that's why she eventually burned herself.

My own attempt

In the years after my father's death, when the inheritance was divided and I lived on my own, I entered into a relationship that lasted for a number of years. After about five years we separated, but in the meantime we had had two children, a son and a daughter. Both children are now in their twenties and I am very grateful that they are doing well and that they have not seen any of the problems my generation has faced.

I was in a relationship for a while after that, but I struggled with that too, because I kept wondering if it was love or some kind of caring that I was only too happy to take advantage of. That conflict grew stronger and at a certain point I couldn't take it anymore. I was also admitted then, just as I was admitted for a while after the previous relationship.

At a certain point I couldn't live with it anymore and I looked for a way to end it; but in such a way that other people would not be bothered by it.

Then one night I tried to gas myself, in a forest, with a bag over my head. At one point as the gas started to take effect on my body, I heard a terrible and persistent beep in my head and with my eyes closed I saw the image of a rapidly spinning disc. I was then saved by my Catholic upbringing, because I suddenly got scared and I thought, suppose this is my eternal punishment, that sound and that image from that disc.

I then pulled that bag off my head with my last strength and when I came to again I saw in my imagination, high above me, the image of my father and mother saying to me: "It is not your time yet".

Peace of Mind

That was of course a very wonderful experience, which has always stayed with me. After this failed attempt I was admitted again, but now for the first time it was a terrible experience. Not only was I conflicted that I wanted to take care of my children and at the same time was very afraid of doing anything, it was also the case that this clinic had a different regime where you would be isolated and tied up if they didn't know how you would behave. No, that was a bad experience.

I have now been living entirely on my own for a number of years now and a certain peace has come over me. This has to do with, among other things, following 14 months of particularly supportive day therapy, the increasing deepening of Connecting Communication and daily doing online Dyad meditations, which I was introduced to a year ago. I experience these aids as particularly healing, so that I dare to stand more and more in my strength and vulnerability and go into life every day with a certainty that

I have not been able to experience all my life. I am extremely grateful for that.

B.C. Peeters is a pseudonym, as the author wishes to protect the privacy of his family.

8

THE SCARS OF WAR

By Jannie Schaffelaar

We were children of war; my two sisters and me. All three of us were born around or during World War II. And I was the middle child of the three of us.

My parents were in their thirties. We lived in Amsterdam and my father was a secondary school teacher. We could have been a happy family if war had not destroyed our lives forever.

The War

In May 1940, the Second World War started for the Netherlands. The Germans occupied our country and the Nazis started their reign of terror. They recruited Dutch boys for forced labor in Germany and they put Jews - men, women and children - on transport to the concentration camps in the East.

I never really knew my father - I was two when he passed away. But, he must have been a righteous and principled person. He could not stand the injustice and violence done to other people and he joined the resistance.

He helped dozens of Jewish families find a hiding place in the polders in the area and we also had Jewish people in hiding at our home.

He will undoubtedly also have committed other acts of resistance. In any case, he was later suspected of the attack on the Amsterdam population register. Thanks to that register, the Nazis were able to trace all Jews in Amsterdam, and that was then made impossible in one fell swoop.

The Jump

Things went wrong in 1943. My father was betrayed and arrested by the Germans. My mother was five months pregnant with my younger sister at the time.

My father knew how gruesome the interrogation techniques of the Germans were. And he realized that eventually he wouldn't be able to keep silent. In doing so, he would endanger the lives of other resistance fighters, as well as the dozens of Jewish families at the hiding places, but also the people who had been hiding them all that time.

The chance that my father would survive his imprisonment, even after a confession, was nil. And, so my father - I think - made the only right decision; however inhumane.

As soon as he saw the opportunity, he did not hesitate for a moment: He jumped down from the third floor of the prison, towards death and freedom.

Widow

And so the war took away my father and the chance for a happy family life. After his death, it would never be the way it was. My younger sister was born four months later. All three of us had to grow up without a father, without a husband in the house.

So halfway through the war, my mother was on her own. A widow with three young children. But, she hardly wanted to accept help from anyone. She felt that asking for help would make her vulnerable. And she didn't want to, because she couldn't be under those circumstances. I do remember, that during the last years of the war - especially during the hunger winter, there was help from the resistance or from the farmers in the polder. One morning we found a pile of sugar beets in the coal shed. They had been put there at night. My mother never spoke about my father, actually. It was literally unmentionable and she kept it up until her death. I remember one moment when there seemed to be an exception. I was a teenager, and my mother seemed to have been advised by a befriended couple to talk to the children about their father. Those people had made it clear to her that children cannot grow up without having some idea of who their father was. My mother then dealt with that very firmly - but also very awkwardly. At one point, she asked all three of us to sit down at the table because she wanted to discuss something with us. We were very curious, but the message was short and uninviting, actually. She said it would be okay if we heard a little more about our father and that we should feel free to ask questions. We were too flabbergasted to come up with questions right away, so the meeting ended. No one came back to that later. For me, the loss of my father mainly meant not having a husband in the house. We were literally a womens' home. And since my mother sought little contact with the outside world, hardly any men came to visit. A single uncle, or a handyman if something needed to be repaired. But that was it. It was only later that I realized how important the interaction between parents is to form a picture of a marriage, of a family. I read many books in my youth, but the image of a family that was described in them was an ideal image that did not really correspond to everyday reality.

Outsider

Everyone in our area knew my father's story. Certainly, in the first years people felt very sorry for the children of the resistance hero. Partly because of this, I felt like an outsider at school. I turned into myself and often felt alone during those years. I tried my best in school and I read a lot of books, but I knew little about the adult world.

First Marriage

With no clear comparison, I had no idea what the ideal man should look like. I didn't know which character traits were important to a good relationship; I didn't really know anything.

And so, I married at far too young an age to a man by no means ideal: The first one who paid me any attention, and that was the man who tutored me in math.

But at the time, I didn't know any better and I tried to make the most of it. With this man I gave birth to two daughters that I raised them with a lot of love.

I also started a career of my own: I tutored at a school for three years, and then I was asked to come and work there as a teacher. I also enjoyed doing that for years. Looking back, it is special that I actually followed in my father's footsteps.

But you shouldn't be teaching all your life, so after a while, I started looking for something else. I eventually became a business journalist and I stayed that way until my retirement.

After my first marriage, I remarried one more time. Although that was not an ideal marriage, it did offer me the opportunity to develop myself more as a person.

I became more social and I enjoyed nature as a place to relax. In my own garden I paid a lot of attention to the blooming of the roses.

Learning

I started painting and always chose nature as an object for painting. During my many travels abroad, I have often used the painting palette. In this way, I was able to make things tangible that initially seemed elusive.

Learning and gaining knowledge have always been very important to me. I mainly wanted to understand things. I have read a lot and also participated in courses and that have brought me to whom I am today.

After the death of my second husband, I felt a lot of relaxation for the first time. I started taking in people, albeit very differently from my father during the war.

I have two grandsons (the women's house now seems very far away), and I think it is important that they are given every opportunity to develop further.

I have come a long way to gain insights, but it has been worth it because I am happy with who I am now.

Jannie Schaffelaar is a pseudonym, as the author wishes to protect the privacy of her family.

9

FOR ME SHE HAD ALREADY DIED
A FEW TIMES

By Mirjam Vijverberg

I was born in 1965 in Delft, a small city in the Netherlands. My first three years we lived in an apartment, but I don't remember any of it. My father told me that it was already difficult for my mother. She was afraid of being left alone. Sometimes she could take good care of me, other times she couldn't and let me cry. Then we moved into a family home. It was a nice great home and I enjoyed playing outside. I was an adventurous kid. If someone said to me: 'You dare not.'….. that was an invitation to do it for sure!! I liked to play with small plastic animals and with my stuffed animals. I created my own story and the animals came to life in my fantasy. My father worked in the debtors-department for five days and my mother was at home. When I was about seven years old, my mother started a shop called 'Pinocchio'. It was a store with homemade clothes and toy animals, with beads and jewellery, antique bottles and jars. At markets and fairs, she could find anything to sell again. We moved and went to live above the shop in the centre of Delft. It was nice to go with my mother to the market, look at things for the store, and have lunch together. But I knew, the day would always end in drama. She was tired, she had a headache, she had bought the wrong things or whatever.... everything was wrong. She went to bed and I didn't know what to do, afraid to do something wrong, afraid of her words, afraid of her eyes.

Rising tension

My mother was very creative. She was creative in her thinking ability, creative with needle and thread, creative with pencil and paint. Creative in organizing parties, everything perfect as she had it in mind. If it went differently, tensions ran high. I remember my sister's First Communion party. The invitations were beautiful, she made a beautiful dress for my sister, the cake was wonderful. But the party could only start when the pastor was also there, which, unfortunately, he had forgotten. Poor little sister, there was to be no party. My mother was lying in bed with a headache and the guests went home. I was very ashamed of events like this. It was difficult to meet the imperative demands of my mother, compelling thoughts of how to live. I had a good relationship with my father. Sometimes I was angry with him because he wasn't there when I needed him. I could say anything to him, cry and scream. We always made up before I went to sleep. That was important for me, that gave me certainty. With my mother there was no certainty. I never knew where I stood. If the certainty fell from my father, I had nothing to fall back on. We understood each other, and that felt good.

When I was nine years old, my sister was born. In the beginning it was special to have a little sister. But soon it all became too much for my mother. My father did a lot in housekeeping and often took care of my sister. Eventually my mother was admitted to a mental health hospital. Various charities came to our house. Some helpers were fun and loving, others were strict and distant. It was not possible to build a normal bond with my mother or my sister. My mother clung to my sister. And together they manipulated our family. That was my sister's way of surviving. She knew exactly how to turn my mother on to have her way. My sister had borderline, she looked for safety, security, reliability in other ways with the necessary consequences.

Survival strategies

Because my mother was often admitted to a psychiatric hospital, was often ill or could not do anything, the shop closed. We moved to another house, just outside the old town. My mother could no longer handle the hustle and bustle of the city. I was thirteen years old and went to school in The Hague, every day taking the tram back and forth from Delft to The Hague. My girlfriend also lived in Delft so we could travel together. Horse riding was very important to me. I wanted nothing more than to have my own horse. I was at the riding school all Saturday. Riding outside on the beach was the best thing there was. No worries, no thrills. But always the excitement of going home, not knowing what my mother would be like. Is there dinner or should I make food? Is it fun or is there tension? I did everything to make my mother happy. If my mother was doing well, it was also fine with me. On Friday evenings, we went to get pastries from the bakery. At the bakery I was always doubting….. "Which pastry does my mother want?" Fearing that I had chosen the wrong pastry for her, I let her choose. And how often did she choose that delicious pastry that I had actually chosen for myself. Everything for a happy mother.

And so, I created survival strategies by thinking ahead, pleasing and being alert. In the evening I sat in front of my large mirror in my room with my dog and went through the day: What was good and fun today and what was not? And then the tears came. I put my arm around my dog and cried, my dog whimpered softly. I didn't understand that nobody saw that I was having a hard time (except my father). No one at school knew. I said nothing about this to others and I did not ask anyone for help. I kept everything to myself and I thought it was almost normal.

Uncertainty

My mother was depressed and lived with fear, insecurity, and voices in her head. Life was hard and complicated and she made her own creation of what was possible for her. The church was her focal point; she made beautiful wall hangings and nativity scenes for the church. There she found peace for a while. It was easier to be in the church community than in her own family. When it was

Christmas, she invited poor people or people with problems to the Christmas dinner. She made a wonderful dinner, but when the people went home, she collapsed completely. And, we, as family had the tension.

She had been admitted to a mental health hospital several times. But the turmoil, fear, and voices in her head did not go away. She took a lot of pills. I never knew what she would be like when I got home. There was always tension about what was to come. Sometimes it was fun, there was tea and tasty cookies but other times she was lying in bed in the dark and nothing was good. This uncertainty was terrible. Her despair grew more and more. If she had too many pills, her voice would be weird and she said weird things.

When I was nineteen years old, I rented an apartment with a friend. There was room for each of us and a common living room and kitchen. My choice of school did not go well. I found it difficult to concentrate and started working - first in a clothing store, then as a dental assistant. And then I painted 'Delft Blue' for 13 years.

Hospital

When my sister was eleven years old she moved to a foster

family. My father divorced my mother after 25 years. He took guilt, shame, and responsibility with him. My mother lived in her own house now; still, my father was often there to help her. She claimed attention, and I felt guilty when I did not visit her often enough. At that time, I lived with my friend. When the phone rang, I was aware that my mother called. Sometimes, she had taken pills and said strange things to my friend when he answered the phone. He wanted to protect me from my mother's constraints and became angry out of impatience. This was so confusing to me. I felt caught between these two persons. A feeling that I had nowhere to go with, as everything I would do or say at that moment would not be right after all.

The first time her stomach had to be pumped I was very shocked and confused: How could my mother do this? After taking a lot of pills she called my father with a voice that was almost impossible to understand. Half of the pills had been absorbed into the blood. She didn't want to die, just have some peace of mind. The tension of whether or not she would survive was very unreal. I think I was sixteen years old. After this first attempt there would be more. She kept saving up the pills. She would also threaten with it: "If you leave, I'll take pills, I can't be alone!" The first time I visited her in the hospital was difficult. The second time was even more difficult. I realised I couldn't do this anymore. I felt exhausted and empty. I sent her a bunch of flowers with a card: 'Sorry, dear Mum, but I'm unable to visit you when you've taken pills.' She accepted this, which I appreciated very much.

I heard these threats the first, and maybe the second, times I visited her in the hospital. But, after that, I felt empty and the threats were without effect.

Funeral

For me, she had already died a few times when she said she had cancer. I was 31 years old and mother of a daughter and a baby boy. Of course, it was sad for my mother but I didn't know how to handle it. At first, the cancer seemed to make her more powerful; it was clear that there was now a disease. I found it difficult to define my role, and I found it difficult to take my own place. My father was divorced from my mother, I was married and had children. My sister was in a special house for people with borderline. My survival strategies were still running at full speed: Thinking ahead, pleasing and being alert. In my own family it didn't work, and my inner critic said: "I can't, I'm doing wrong, I don't know, I don't matter and I do everything on my own." Eventually, my mother was moved to a nursing home. I felt guilty because I didn't visit her often, but I couldn't. I felt guilty because I couldn't support her and give her understanding. I felt that I was playing it. I was afraid that if she died she wanted me to hold her hand. When that moment came, I was able to and it was good. It was the quiet part before her death. And then the compelling eyes came again, I had to take things but did not understand her. She became more and more compelling. I left, the nurses and my husband took over. There was a battle against death, I had allowed her a quiet death. I wasn't there when she died. I shouldn't have left!

It rained and stormed on the day of her funeral. I was pregnant with our third daughter. My mother wanted to be buried in a bare wooden coffin with a cotton sheet around her instead of a shiny chest with a lace cloth. (She said: "When I'm dead I don't want to be in a candy box.") I have not been able to make this happen. Throughout the funeral I felt my mother's eyes, the feeling that I hadn't done well. Grief and loss can comfort you, but guilt and shame cannot; I felt lonely and misunderstood. Guilty because I wasn't there when she died, guilty because of the coffin, ashamed because I didn't miss her and wasn't sad.

My own way

I have had to learn that I am not dependent on the reaction
and opinions of others. I have had to learn that I can rely on
myself with all my beautiful and less beautiful sides. All
my accumulated beliefs have made me who I am today. I
have recognized and accepted them. They helped me
survive, but then they became a burden to me. It was
difficult to really connect with myself. I have learned to get
closer to my inner child, to cherish and comfort her when
she is sad. I let her know that she matters, that she can ask
for help and that she doesn't have to do everything alone.
That takes time, patience, and energy - and doesn't work
every day. My beliefs have softened and narrowed. They
will always remain triggered, but they no longer prevail.
There is room now to develop new talents and to live life
with passion.

Everyone acted according to their own abilities and
possibilities. I hated it when people said I looked like my
mother; being afraid of having the same genes as her. I'm
afraid that my children have the same genes as her. I have
been very ashamed of my mother to my partner. But
everyone takes his or her luggage from childhood. Life
goes on and my mother can be here now. I inherited her

creativity, her care, her interest in books, her cooking skills, her passion for nature and spirituality, but in my own way!!

That makes me happy!

Every child wants to be seen, every child wants to get attention. My sister demanded attention and love in a way because she did not get the attention and love she craved. Her emergency measures were high with dire consequences. Other people and loved ones also suffered from this. As a child I kept it to myself, others did not see it. I got my attention and love by being good to others. There are so many children trying to get what they didn't get from their parents. I want to mean something to these children. When I was 37 years old, I was a primary school teacher. There are so many children in a class who want extra attention, I couldn't give that. I wanted to help the children individually. I started my own practice "Child Coach Met Stip". I still work in a primary school, but not as a teacher. I help children individually with the subject matter with attention to the whole child. I am interested in the background of the child and try to help with what the child needs. It is not only the child who needs help, also the parents. I try to help them together. And that makes me happy!

I was born and raised in the Netherlands, in the beautiful old town of Delft. I am married and I have three children, a dog and a cat. After having painted 'Delft Blue' for more than ten years and the experiences I have had with my own children, the desire came to work professionally with children. When I was 37 years old I started working as a primary school teacher. I saw myself in the children who needed extra help and attention. This made it difficult to work as a classroom teacher. But it opened doors to work with children individually. Through my own experiences in my childhood I can connect with the child. I started my own children's coach practice "Kindercoach met Stip".

In order to really be there for the child I learned to really be there for myself. That's how I discovered Ofkje Teekens' 'Young Talent' game. And so I became a Young Talent coach. My dream is to work in schools with the Talent game, to bring children in contact with themselves in a playful way: Who am I? What do I want? And what do I dream of? To make them believe in their own abilities and let their talents and qualities shine. I work mostly with children, but also with (young) adults. I work with them individually but also in workshops or in a group.

https://www.kindercoachmetstip.com

10

STILL CONNECTED

By Marjet van der Wal

I started counting October 24, 2015. Five years ago, Benjamin chose to step out of his life. Benjamin was my lover. Everything seemed to stand still. Then the counting started. First the hours; then the days, then the weeks, and then the months.

And now, with the years, I don't really "count" anymore.

There are many stories about Benjamin, and Benjamin's death. So diverse and very different. This is my story; my story with Benjamin.

The big differences in the stories are also due to Benjamin himself. He was a boy of many faces.

Many faces

With friends, he was completely different than when with family, within the family different to everyone, and different at work. To me, it seemed like he was part of all faces. At times, I could glimpse the beautiful man he was, although he was hiding behind all those faces.

Everyone is different, when you are in a different company, that's how it goes. Only, with Benjamin, it went further. Many people did not know who he really was or how he was doing, that it was just one of the faces he had.

Even when I lived with him, I couldn't always tell how he was really doing.

Benjamin and I had a deep relationship, like a fierce storm whose wind was wonderfully fresh, and you could warm your cheek at the same time. Where the sun could shine and with the blink of your eyes it could be pouring down with rain.

Looking into his eyes, we could get lost in deep black valleys and emerge together in the radiant sun.

I was not afraid of his black thoughts, not afraid of his longing for death, and not afraid of the beautiful power that was hidden within him.

Those two extremes lived in him. There was pain, but still beauty; all at the same time. Somehow, we understood each other in that.

It touched a feeling, that sometimes made me feel inseparable from him. So strong, that I could lose myself in him.

I realized that relationship a while before his death. We were swallowed up by our love, but, somehow, with feelings like it wasn't right. I tried to distance myself.

That day

That day I tried in vain. Several times, we called each other, argued like only we could argue, and at the back of that argument I felt how much I loved him.

October 24, 2015, at 10.30 pm, he cuts off our telephone conversation with the words: "So this will be the evening." At that point, I don't realize what it's about, because our fight was about his fear of losing me. I sent him a message about that.

Forty-five minutes later, I see a photo on Facebook with words underneath that should act as a goodbye. But these words are not goodbyes. These words are a slap in the face. A stab in my heart.

At 11:15 pm you left this world without saying goodbye.

That night, it seems like I can cry harder than the shower can poor. The week looks like a big thick fog has risen around me. I can only take mini steps in search of something that should resemble life.

Then the counting starts. The hours, 1 day, 2 days, 3 days, a week, 2 weeks ... a month, three months, your birthday, half a year, 7 months, almost your death day ... a year ...

A year, that I have come through with friends, family, and in a place where it feels like I am still surrounded by its warmth.

A friend has put my feet on the ground again and again. By taking me to concerts, eating out, and giving all the space to my grief. Strange timing for a "romance", and yet it has drawn me back to life, time and time again. It made me bear this intense grief.

That year, I was not a nice person to my colleagues, among others; I was a perfectionist.

I was someone who could not cope with change; I was full of grief, frustration, and anger. Besides taking on the "task" that was urged on me in a farewell letter from Benjamin.

This suicide note is dated April 2015, a time when he had previously faced the choice. He wrote: "There is something brewing in you that is about to burst. And once you explode, the world will be flooded with love. I hope you will still do that for me. Also give away my love."

Because of this, I wanted to take over the work so well, the work that was also his "life's work". It made me very passionate and a perfectionistic. The performances were not allowed to stop. Not like Benjamin had quit. We had to keep reaching and helping the youth. Benjamin was fantastic at his job. The audience didn't have to explain to him what it is like to wear something this big or have dark feelings and thoughts.

Questions

After his death, there were many questions about what I knew and what it was like.

How could Benjamin get out of life when he was so passionate about our work to help young people not to?

Gradually, I got the feeling that there might be a few other people besides me whom he had allowed into his inner world. Those who had seen him with all the different "faces" he had. I often feel very alone in my grief for

Benjamin as I knew him.

In his farewell letter, he also wrote: "You have to keep moving, always keep moving forward. Movement is good." And that's what I do. Literally and figuratively. I continue from one work to another. With friends who are close to me, I reflect on the figurative movement within myself. With the help of a grief counselor, I gain more and more insight into how my grief moves within me, and what it does to me.

The counting continues, and so does life. About 1 year after his death, I met a new love again. A man who was friend to Benjamin's sister, and brother-in-law. He had seen Benjamin before, but I did not know him. Once, they both helped his sister move.

Benjamin's words about my new love still move me: "What a good boy that is."

These words bring a kind of peace to the situation. No endorsement, it makes it quiet, and maybe, a little easier.

Then, a life begins with a new love, and the grief of the loss of Benjamin side by side. This life is increasingly starting to balance. I start coming back to my "old me" more and more. I laugh at the smallest things again, a sparkle goes through my body when I see a fruit fall from the maple.

I chat again with the unknown cats I meet on the street. The shape of my grief keeps changing. I become more resilient.

Counting flies. We count the years. One, two, three, four, five.

Five.

Five years later.

Five years ago, I said to Benjamin: "It is not the love that changes, but the form. We have made a heart connection -- from heart to heart.

It was the shape that changed, not our love. Now, you have changed the shape again, for everyone, forever."

Still connected

I still feel that connection from heart to heart. It is still there. I believe it will always be there. Sometimes, that feeling is in the form of an intensity within my heart; sometimes, it's there in the form of an abundance of tears; sometimes, I feel a great loss; I can sense it in a beautiful sky, and sometimes, in a gigantic laugh! This commitment is so valuable. It's strange to say; I am so grateful to Benjamin for showing and feeling this connection. Now, five years later, I can say that. I found my resilience somewhere, found the movement of my life. Keep moving forward. I am (still) moving around the theme of mourning. Soon I will start a course for grief counseling for children. I discovered that interest through his death. Now, five years later, I have become a mother to an 11 month old son. I have discovered that the world of happiness can exist in addition to my sadness.

The roots of my life lie in Friesland, in the north of the

Netherlands. In my 31 year old life I have lived in many places. From Denmark and Groningen, to long summers in Limburg. For a number of years this has been the place where I found my home again. A home with a sweet husband and an 11-month-old son.

From my 17th to my 21st I trained to become a Theatre Teacher. Then I started as an entrepreneur in the cultural sector. I worked as a teacher of extracurricular arts, director on major projects in the church community of the village where I grew up and as an actress in various places, including Theatre Traxx and Studio Tape. At Theatre Traxx I played for 8 years in performances at secondary education, and at MBO and HBO courses. These performances have themes like Grief and Loss, Depression and peer pressure / alcohol abuse.

At Studio Tape we have created the children's performance "I see, I see, what you see" to make death easier for children to discuss. A visual listening performance for anyone who sometimes misses someone.

Since this year I have been teaching at "Havingness", a center for intuitive development. I supervise the first year and, together with other teachers, offer a place to look for answers in yourself, in a playful way.

A grounded, warm and trusted place where I have been able to develop myself over the past 5 years, and where I have been able to find resilience and confidence in myself.

In 2021, at the institute "Het Land van Rouw", I will start a course for grief counseling with an outflow profile of "children". In the future I hope to be able to start a practice for children and to guide them in their grief.

ON PREVENTION

As suicide is recognized worldwide as a major health problem, more and more prevention programs are being developed. According to the World Health Organization (WHO) 40 countries have a national prevention program. And as the WHO states, that's far too few and much more is needed.

This gap is filled by local initiatives and NGO's, supported by government grants and many, many volunteers.

Many countries of the world have a national telephone number that people can phone whenever they are depressed, have suicidal thoughts or feel lonely. Most of these lines can be used any time of day or night, 24/7.

www.en.wikipedia.org/wikilist_of_suicide_crisis_lines

presents a list of all known and active suicide-crisis-lines in the world.

In the United Kingdom

https://www.nhs.uk/conditions/suicide/ shows contact information of the 'Samaritans', the 'Campaign Against Living Miserably (CALM)' especially for men, and other organizations working for the prevention of suicide.

In the Netherlands it is: www.113.nl

In Flanders (North Belgium) it is: www.zelfmoord1813.be

And in the USA it is: www.suicide.org

Most of these national organizations participate in international organizations like:

European Alliance against Depression (www.eaad.net)
Or the International Association for Suicide Prevention (www.iasp.info)

Anyone having feelings of depression or suicidal thoughts, can contact the national organizations 24 hours a day, seven days a week. Anyone worried or concerned about someone who has these feelings, can contact these organizations as well.

ABOUT THE AUTHORS

Ofkje Teekens is a Jungian Psychologist, a Talent-coach and trainer, a transformational teacher, an international speaker and a published author.

www.ofkjeteekens.com

Kees M. Paling is a cultural sociologist, a writer, a journalist, a communication consultant and a writing coach.

www.keesmpaling.com